"This is one of those jewels you don't want to place down until you've reached the final page. It's about character and inspiration and reminds me of a talk the late North Carolina State basketball coach Jim Valvano gave when he was dying of cancer: 'Don't give up–don't ever give up!' Levin was inspired by many cases of owner dedication and canine fortitude and details those beautifully in this upbeat book that accents heroism, attitude and inspiration."

Ranny Green
Seattle Times

"Well-written, uplifting and inspirational, not only is "Blind Dog Stories" a wonderful illustration of the human-canine bond, but it is a testimony to the quality of life a blind dog can enjoy and enhance for his owner. I could have gone on reading these great dog stories forever!"

Sandra Mueller
Associate Editor for The Living Chow Chow

"These stories illustrate that some dogs will not only cope with blindness but flourish if given the chance. I believe this new book will give owners the courage to give their pets that opportunity."

Richard Christmas DVM
Canadian Association of Veterinary Ophthalmology

Blind Dog Stories

Tales of Triumph, Humor and Heroism

Caroline D. Levin R.N.

 Lantern Publications

Third Printing, September 2001
Printed in Canada

🏮 Lantern Publications
18709 S. Grasle Road
Oregon City, OR 97045

ISBN: 0-9672253-1-0
LCCN: 2001116527

Cover photographs courtesy of:

(Top) : John Zamora
(Center) : Randy Cooper - sled team
Tim Luchsinger - Golden Retriever
(Bottom) : AnneMarie Haden

Dedication

This book is dedicated in memory of:

"Liebschen"
Dornlea's Blithe Spirit CDX
1991-1998

While she was not a blind dog, I could certainly tell a few stories about her. She was my companion, protector, and best girl; and I wanted to honor her life.

This book is also dedicated to Dottie, Targa, Butterscotch and Lumpur. Whether their lifetime stories are cut short, or play out in full, they all leave us much too soon.

Acknowledgements

Thanks to my husband, Daniel, for suggesting this project in the first place, and for his talent and assistance. Thanks to my generous friends: Patty Bonnstetter and Joe Megaw, for technical assistance. And of course many thanks to the blind-dog owners who shared their stories with the rest of us:

Jamie, Harry and "Jenilyn"
Annette, Steve, Paul and "Norman"
Zelda and "Samantha"
Kathy and "Keller"
Stephanie, Buddy and "Charlotte"
Richard, Barbara and "Butterscotch"
Donna and "Trinket"
Connie, John and "Dottie"
Susie, Chris, "Lumpur" and "Radar"
Pam and "Daisy"
Sher, Morris and "Bobbie Sue"
Julie, Tim and "Charlie"
Gail, Shelby, Chris and "Crackers"
Angele, Jim and "Carlisle"
Gudrun, James and "Maedchen"
Linda and "Tyler"
AnneMarie, Gary and "Pippy"
Jan, Mark and "Hogan"
Anne, Charles and "Targa"

Contents

Preface

When I wrote my first book, *"Living With Blind Dogs"* I was privileged to meet many blind dogs and their owners. These people proudly told me tales of their dogs' deeds—from day-to-day success stories and adventures to acts of true heroism.

I learned two particular points from these conversations. First, I realized that some people react to canine blindness with plans to euthanize or abandon their dogs. I must admit I did not realize the prevalence of this reaction. These dog owners mistakenly believe that a blind dog's life must be a miserable existence or that training one would be an insurmountable task. This is not true and I wanted to publicize it. Second, I learned that the owners of newly blinded dogs took great comfort in hearing the success stories of others, those who had already conquered their fears and grief and whose dogs were living normal and happy lives.

I've written this book, *"Blind Dog Stories,"* to address these two points, to illustrate that blind dogs do lead full lives, and to offer comfort to the owners of newly-blinded-dogs. These stories come from all around the world, and depict actual events.

Hearing these remarkable tales has further deepened my respect for dogs and canine behavior. I am continually amazed at the strength of the human-canine bond, even in the face of blinding illnesses and injuries. I think you will be, too. Show me a blind dog in a good home, and I will introduce you to some of the best people on Earth.

*"Shared joy is double joy,
shared sorrow is half sorrow."*

— Swedish proverb

Blind Enthusiasm

mush-er, *n.* One who trains and races sled dogs.

Gang-line, *n.* A polypropylene rope that connects the dogs to the sled.

Jen-i-lyn, *n.* A blind Siberian Husky.

in-spir-a-tion-al, *a.* Jenilyn.

I n the dog fancy, Taaneth is described as a "dilute black with an open face." In other words, she is a Siberian Husky with a black top-coat and creamy-white undercoat. Together they give her the appearance of being almost gray. Her face is white without dark markings. And at the time she was pregnant with her first litter, Taaneth lived at one of Alaska's pre-

Photo courtesy of Jamie West

mier sled-racing kennels—a kennel with a 50-year history of breeding top Siberian Huskies.

Each winter, mushers travel to this kennel to work and learn the tricks of the trade: kennel management, sled racing, and breeding world-class Siberians. The pay is low, but the experience is invaluable. This year's group of mushers included three girls named Jennifer, Jenni and Eveline.

During an otherwise uneventful pregnancy, and unbeknownst to the mushers, Taaneth had developed a serious abdominal infection. On the night she went into labor, the three girls watched her closely. They could see that Taaneth was having a difficult labor and called the veterinarian. When the doctor arrived, he immediately performed a Caesarian Section.

Three of the six puppies did not survive the birth. The peritonitis was passed on to a fourth puppy in the form of a severe eye infection. This would ultimately leave the puppy with very little sight. After an already-emotional delivery, the veterinarian announced in a thick voice that Taaneth was dying. He did not expect her to live much longer.

Jennifer, Jenni and Eveline immediately devoted themselves to this newly-formed family of dogs. They took turns bottle-feeding the puppies and nursing Taaneth back to health. The girls took a special liking to the blind puppy, both in spite of, and because of, her handicap. Her curious puppy nature disguised the fact that she had little useful vision.

The mushers found the blind puppy exactly the kind of new owners she would need—people who were good-natured and tolerant—really, what any puppy needs. The girls couldn't have done better than when they found Jamie and her husband, Harry, a local Alaskan couple.

As soon as the puppy arrived in Jamie's home, she named her in tribute to the three mushers. "Jen", "Jenni" and "Eveline" became "Jenilyn". As Jamie and Harry explain, "Jenilyn would not even be here if not for these girls."

At that time, Jamie and Harry owned a variety of other dogs, most of them true working sled dogs. "Each year, we're willing to accept deserving additions into our pack," as Jamie puts it. "This year, it was Jenilyn."

And, while overall, this was an agreeable placement for this puppy, Jenilyn's arrival wasn't without its share of emotion. As Jamie reminisces, "The first day she came to us, she was bouncing around, learning to navigate through the chair rungs. My husband cried. It was so sad for him to think of us having a little blind pup. Meanwhile, Jenilyn could not have cared less."

Harry was also a little concerned about how Jenilyn would survive the often "every man for himself" mentality of a multi-sled-dog home. He was afraid the other dogs would pick on the puppy. "Instead, she bossed the other dogs around and pushed past things that got in her way," Jamie explains.

Unfortunately, Jenilyn continued to have eye problems. She developed painful glaucoma, which necessitated the surgical removal of one eye, all this when she was just eight weeks old. Five months later, the puppy's remaining eye became painful too. Jamie and Harry made the decision to have a silicone sphere implanted in that eye. While this procedure retained the cosmetic appearance of her eye, nothing could be done to restore her vision.

Photo courtesy of Jamie West

As a young adult, Jenilyn was totally blind. One eye retained a normal appearance but had no vision; the other eye was sewn closed. And the result: It gave the distinct impression that Jenilyn was winking...a humorous, mischievous wink that pretty well summed up what Jenilyn was all about.

From the start, Jamie made an effort to build her puppy's self-assurance. Jamie recalls, "Whether that meant doing a six-inch recall in the living room for a hotdog or guiding her through the house with the leash, my primary objective was to further boost Jenilyn's confidence." It worked.

One summer morning, Jamie stood at the fence talking to her neighbor Randy. As they talked, Jenilyn trotted through the maze of trees, wiggled over to the couple, and jumped up and down for attention. Randy leaned over and asked, "Do you know she has her eye closed?"

Jamie thought to herself, "No kidding, that ain't all!" In fact, Jamie (who is a long-time dog handler and experienced in canine behavior) admits that Jenilyn continually surprises her.

Once, Jamie took the young dog out for a walk and Jenilyn jumped into the air after a butterfly. "I remember thinking at the time, 'how cute.' Then I remembered that she couldn't be doing things like that, but she *was*!" puzzles Jamie.

Another afternoon, Jamie witnessed their house cat racing down the stairs with Jenilyn in hot pursuit. At the

Photo courtesy of Jamie West

bottom of the stairs, the cat took a hard, 90-degree turn. Jenilyn followed suit, her feet comically sliding on the hardwood floors. Jamie's mouth dropped. "It certainly didn't look like a maneuver any blind dog would do!"

Jamie is not alone in this reaction. Like anyone else on a routine trip to the vet's office, Jamie and Jenilyn were called from the waiting room. Jenilyn ran down the hall at a gallop, rounded the corner and jumped onto the waiting veterinary tech. The girl laughed, and asked if anything was wrong with her. Jamie, feeling mischievous, grinned and said, "No. Nothing's wrong with her. She's just blind." Jamie remembers the technician's shocked, double take. It's a look that many blind-dog owners come to know.

As Jenilyn got older, she began to help Jamie with her chores. "I got tired of her always jumping up to 'see' what I was doing or carrying, so I taught her the 'It's mine' command," explains Jamie. In fact, Jamie believed that her blind dog was doing so well learning new skills that she decided to try an experiment. She wanted to see if Jenilyn would enjoy pulling the sled.

"Now, it's important to realize that serious sled dog training doesn't begin until a dog is a year old or more," Jamie explains. "Any earlier and it can inhibit and damage bone growth. However, it can be advantageous to start a young dog to develop the 'fun' of working. In Jenilyn's case, it was a way to teach her that when she was in the harness, it was completely safe for her to lean forward, and go, go, go!" What could more fun and rewarding for a young animal bred to pull and race?

Jamie fashioned a gangline to the stem of her bicycle. To the front of the line she hooked up Murphy, her lead dog. She calls Murphy "Mr. Perfect Leader" because he keeps the line pulled out straight and taut. Jamie knew Murphy would be a good choice for this experiment because he would not pull Jenilyn over or come around to visit Jamie on her bike.

Next, she attached Jenilyn to the gangline behind Murphy. Jenilyn was attached in two places, or "points", one called a "neckline" and the other called a "tugline." The neckline connects a dog to the main line by the collar. The tugline connects the dog from the back of the harness near the tail and transfers all the pulling power. Jamie also hung a little bell on Murphy's harness so Jenilyn would be able to hear him running ahead of her.

Photo courtesy of Harry West

By this point, Murphy was so excited to be off that his toenails were scraping the asphalt. Jamie slowly eased off the bicycle's brakes. She watched Jenilyn closely as they started off and noticed that Jenilyn was using the gangline as a reference point, feeling for it and using it to keep herself straight. "It was something I hadn't thought of, but since it ran taut beside her, it was easy for Jenilyn to find," explains Jamie.

By the end of the very slow, one-mile run, Jenilyn had figured everything out. Her neckline remained loose (she was keeping pace with Murphy) and her tugline was tight. She, too, was pulling the bike! When they came to a stop, Jenilyn was leaning into her harness, waiting, panting and smiling broadly. The experiment was a huge success. In Jamie's words, "She had a blast!"

These days, Jenilyn runs on Jamie's five-dog recreational team. Jamie takes this team on a three-mile run several times weekly and reports that Jenilyn does remarkably well.

Photo courtesy of Harry West

"In fact, I've even used her as co-lead, attached to another leader. As long as another dog is there to keep her on the trail, she is bound and determined to go forward and 'see' what's out there."

Jamie sums up her experiences this way: "Jenilyn is a very spoiled dog, but by the same token, my expectations of her are very high. When I see her solving problems and acting so normal, it makes me want to encourage other blind-dog owners. I want them to do more than just *accept* their dog's handicap. I want to encourage them to deal with the situation through training and retraining. It seems so bizarre to me when people say that they can't imagine a blind dog having a quality life. They need to meet Jenilyn."

"Nothing great was ever achieved without enthusiasm."

— Ralph Waldo Emerson

To Look in the Face of Danger

Lumpur was a cross between a Golden Retriever and a Labrador. He looked most like a black Lab with a feathery ruff around his neck. He was also a young boy's first dog—a boy named Chris.

Photo courtesy of Susie Sharp

Lumpur came to Chris and his family when he was five months old. He was a sweet, loving dog, but he was completely unsocialized. He had the bad habit of running away when off the leash. Catching him required all of Chris's patience and ingenuity.

Chris and his family can recall few specific changes in Lumpur's behavior over the years, so they are uncertain as to exactly when he began losing his sight. As Lumpur matured though, his retinas were degenerating. Month by month Lumpur, was indeed, going blind.

"When Lump was about three years old," recalls Chris, "he barked viciously at a fire hydrant. Thinking back, that was probably one of the first indications that he couldn't see well. By the time Lumpur was four and partially blind, he still ran away periodically, but it was easy to catch him. It wasn't until we were up close to him that he realized we were about to nab him," Chris grins. In spite of skirmishes like these, Lumpur was truly devoted to his young master.

Chris and his parents were avid campers, and despite the blindness, Lumpur was always included in these trips. When Lumpur was about five years old and Chris about 10, the two set out together to explore the wilderness around their southern Washington picnic area.

"While my father was making sandwiches, Lumpur and I headed off to stretch our legs. I wanted to check out some ground squirrels I had seen along a line of poplar trees," Chris explains. "As I pushed through the brush, my father called out for me to be careful. He said rattle-snakes sometimes co-habitate with those squirrels."

No sooner were those words spoken, when Chris froze, one foot in mid-air. The boy had surprised a large rattle-snake, sunning himself only moments before. The snake was now poised and ready to strike. Chris yelled, "Da-a-a-ad! A rattler!!"

What happened next, took only seconds. Lumpur raced across the field, to join Chris at his side. As Chris slowly set his foot down, the hair on Lumpur's back quickly stood up.

In a blur, Lumpur sprang between the boy and the snake. The rattler was willing to take on any foe and lunged for the dog. Lumpur dodged from side to side. Many times the two danced, and each time the dog avoided the rattler's strike. Chris was motionless, too amazed to move or speak.

Finally, it was Lumpur's turn to strike. He lunged for the snake, catching it by the head. Lumpur shook the snake repeatedly until he was sure it was dead. Just then, Chris' father arrived with a shovel in his hand, but the job was done.

"Lumpur had always hated snakes with a passion," Chris explains. "All his life he had killed snakes, even little garter snakes. Blindness had not diminished this pursuit in any way." Chris continues, "I was truly terrified that day. That was a very large snake in the eyes of a small boy. Lumpur shook it so hard, it flew apart in two pieces!"

In hindsight, Chris says he believes that he would have surely been bitten if Lumpur had not intervened. "Since we were many miles from even the closest hospital, I credit Lump with saving my life."

Shortly after that episode, Lumpur walked off a small cliff. Luckily the ground was sandy and soft, and Lumpur was not hurt. For Chris and his family, this fall confirmed that Lumpur had only a little peripheral vision remaining when he killed the snake.

Photo courtesy of Susie Sharp

Years later, when Chris was away at college, Lumpur was lost to cancer. To this day, Chris sometimes feels badly that he couldn't be there to say goodbye and hold his best friend. Instead, Chris asked his father to hold the phone to Lumpur's head so he could tell his dog how much he loved him.

"Lumpur was a great dog. When he died, he left a huge hole in Chris's heart," explains Chris' new bride, Susie. "That hole is filled now by our new dog, Radar."

Radar is a black Lab. Radar is also blind.

"It's not the size of the dog in the fight, it's the size of the fight in the dog."

-Mark Twain

Seeing is Believing

A t the high-tech company where Susie works, an e-mail bulletin board is provided for employee use. On any given day, it may include advertisements for cars, sporting goods, baby clothes and various other items. One day, it included an ad that read: "Special-Needs Black Lab."

"The first time I saw the notice, I told my then-fiancé, Chris, about it. Ever since I'd known Chris, I knew he felt incomplete without a dog. Losing Lumpur had left an empty spot in his life. We talked about the ad, but decided that someone else would probably take the dog," recalls Susie. "When the ad came out a second time, I gave the phone number to Chris and told him to call."

Susie continues, "A lengthy phone call followed, and we learned the story of this sweet dog. He had been born with a severe condition that resulted in retinal detachment. The vet felt certain that the dog was blind at six to eight weeks of age when he was dumped at the animal shelter to be euthanized." Luckily, the puppy was rescued from the shelter, but a year and a half later, he faced more obstacles. Kirsten, his first owner, was preparing to marry and move away.

Susie explains, "I know she really didn't want to put him up for adoption. She told us that he was like a child to her. I was getting ready to marry too, but my circumstances were very different. Chris needed a dog in his life. This would be my gift to him."

Susie and Chris went to see the Black Lab. "His name was Radar, and he tugged at our heartstrings," says Susie. "Chris hoped he might somehow be able to repay Lumpur's loyalty by helping out another blind dog. Personally, this was my first dog and I was more than a little apprehensive," she grins, "but I got over that."

Susie and Radar have spent many hours together and have bonded closely. Almost every day they visit their favorite spot, an unmown field adjacent to a glider club.

"It's a fascinating place for dogs," says Susie. In the warm months, the lowlands furnish large, deep puddles that are a special pleasure for thirsty dogs; and when the weather turns nasty, waterfowl tuck into the brush to avoid the storms.

"Many times Radar and I are the only ones there. He could spend hours retrieving the plastic bumper that I throw for him to fetch. Radar retrieves very well for a blind dog," Susie explains. "Sometimes, when there *are* other dogs there, Radar even beats a sighted dog to the bumper!"

Another regular visitor to the field is a man who brings his Springer Spaniels to run. One day he stood a short distance away and silently watched as Susie repeatedly threw Radar's bumper, and he happily returned it to her.

Photo courtesy of Susie Sharp

After some time, he came forward and asked Susie why Radar didn't head straight for the bumper, but instead, sniffed around for it.

"I told him that Radar was blind, and that he was using his sense of smell to find it. The man did not believe me," recalls Susie. "He told me I must be mistaken and actually started arguing with me! He contended that Radar had just jumped over a puddle, so he must, in fact, be able to see light and shadows."

Susie explained the details of Radar's history and medical condition to the Spaniel owner. "I told the man it was impossible for Radar to see, that he had detached retinas." The man watched a little longer, shook his head, and marched away.

"I guess it makes some people uncomfortable to think that a blind dog can function so normally. They think I'm trying to fool them. Other people are just surprised that he can actually run, retrieve, and be such a happy dog. They want to talk about what a wonderful dog Radar is, and I'm always willing to do that!" Susie grins.

She continues, "Now I don't tell people that Radar's blind until they've watched him a little bit. If they react like the man with the Springer Spaniels did, I lean over, lower my voice, and whisper, 'It's okay. He doesn't know he's blind'."

"If we are unwilling to be aware of the dark,
we cannot see the light."

— John Cowan

A Different Point of View

Most of us are familiar with the phrase "from out of the mouths of babes" to mean that honesty comes with innocence. With few pre-conceived ideas, children can usually look past flaws and see a greater good. This is a perspective that adults sometimes lack. — C.L.

After many years, Daisy's long battle with eye disease finally came to a close. The veterinarian suggested that it was time to treat Daisy's red, painful eyes, more aggressively. Pam, Daisy's owner, agreed. This meant enucleation — removal of the eyes.

"The idea of putting her down was never even an option for me!" Pam announces. She instructed the veterinarian to proceed with surgery. She wanted to free Daisy from her constant pain.

Pam explains that while it was a difficult decision to make, she and Daisy are both pleased with the choice. "Daisy feels so much better now. Her attitude improved tremendously! She must have been so uncomfortable before the procedure. Now she's back to her old self."

Photo courtesy of Pam Hunt

In fact, the fuzzy white Poodle feels so much better now, that she happily accompanies Pam and her canine brother, Symi, to their local park again. Here, meadows trace the path of Australia's Swan River, providing recreation for dog-lovers and picnickers alike.

Photo courtesy of Pam Hunt

"I love taking my dogs to the park, even though it is sometimes quite an adventure." She giggles, then elaborates,

"Daisy may not be able to see, but she can smell a chicken bone from the other side of the park! Many times she has bolted until she's found the source of the smell, walking over people, picnic baskets, and spilling drinks to get there. Usually the chase ends with Daisy sticking her head onto someone's plate, their fork hovering in mid-air!"

Photo courtesy of Pam Hunt

Pam chuckles again "People usually have a good laugh, and then realize that although Daisy is studying their lunch with such intensity, she really isn't *looking* at them at all! I have to be honest and say that some people have been a little bit alarmed when they see her, but that's not usually the case.

"The funniest comment I ever heard from what I assumed to be a normally intelligent person was: 'Can she still walk?' The worst comment was from a woman who accused me of being cruel for keeping a blind dog alive. I guess *she* couldn't see too well either, because there was Daisy, bouncing up and down, free of pain, and thrilled to be alive. I gave up trying to talk to those kinds of people.

"My favorite story, though, is about my neighbor's daughter, Amelia. She is three years old, very confident, and not afraid of dogs in the least. I meet her father and some of my other neighbors down at the park, every night of the week, come rain or shine."

One evening, about two weeks after Daisy's surgery, Amelia accompanied her father to the park, and got her first good look at Daisy. At that point, Daisy still had stitches, and her hair was only just beginning to grow back. Amelia bent down, pressing her little hands against her knees, and took a hard look into Daisy's face.

Amelia asked, "Why did you have Daisy's eyes taken out?" There was no shock or horror in her voice, just puzzlement.

Pam replied, "Daisy's eye's were sick and since she couldn't see anyway, we took away the pain."

Amelia studied Daisy's face for a few minutes longer. When her attention span ran out, she stood up and announced, "That's fine," and turned away.

Amelia's father started to laugh. He saw the puzzled look on Pam's face and explained, "I reckon some of her dolls will be minus their eyes tomorrow morning!"

S her never thought twice about offering her love to Bobbie Sue...

Photo courtesy of Sher Wardrip

a six-inch tall, three-pound, long-haired, Chihuahua. Bobbie Sue was born without eyes. "She has taught me so much about dealing with the dirty tricks that life can play," says Sher. "She is my inspiration, and I love her dearly.

"Because she is so tiny, we often take her shopping with us," Sher continues. "There are a number of dog-friendly stores near us, and the people there have gotten to know Bobby Sue quite well," Sher smiles. "Children often approach us to see the 'baby doggy', as they describe her."

Sher stops for a moment to think. "Typically, it's the parents who notice that there's something unusual about Bobby Sue's face," she says. "When I explain that she was born without eyes, the children come up with some interesting remarks.

"One little boy asked if there was an operation where she could 'get some'. One little boy tried to reassure me," Sher chuckles. "He said, 'don't worry, when she gets big, they'll grow in'. Another child speculated that 'maybe they were just closed real tight.'"

Photo courtesy of Sher Wardrip

Sher concludes, "Children seem to take Bobby Sue's blindness in stride. More often, it's the adults who have a difficulty accepting that she is okay, so I try to spend a few minutes talking with them." Sher laughs again. "People…you gotta love 'em."

*"Children are remarkable
for their intelligence and ardor,
for their curiosity,
their tolerance of shams,
the clarity and ruthlessness of their vision."*

— Aldous Huxley

Blind Devotion

S amantha was almost 10 years old, the day she came from Grateful Dog Rescue to live with Zelda and her family. Right from the start, Samantha's sweet temperament was apparent.

"She has always been very gentle, easy-going and full of love," Zelda explains. But even so, Zelda realized that she had adopted a dog with special needs. The veterinarian had diagnosed this little 20-pound Terrier-Corgi mix with the beginnings of cataracts.

At first, Samantha was unaware of her own deteriorating vision. She settled into a life of comfort and mutual devotion with her new owner. One of their shared pleasures was a twice-weekly trip to Fort Funston Park, part of the Golden Gate National Recreation Area. Located along the California coast near San Francisco, Fort Funston is described as "a haven for dogs," and aptly so.

From the parking lot, paved pathways wind down one side of a mountain and return from around the other. There are certain spots where dogs and owners can wander down to the beach. And there are many grassy acres, dotted with trees, where dogs are permitted to run free and play off leash. Zelda has been taking her dogs to Fort Funston long before it became the popular dog-park it is today.

Photo courtesy of Zelda Barnard

Samantha came to know every inch of this park. She would romp with her canine friends, sniff new companions in greeting, and trudge through the thick local foliage called "ice plant" in pursuit of interesting scents.

Zelda and Samantha took leisurely strolls around the mountain and even hiked down the steep cliff to reach the beach from time to time. For each of them, these trips to the park were their way of "stopping to smell life's roses." They found pleasure in socializing with friends and in nature's beauty.

As the years passed, Samantha lost more and more of her vision. An infection, followed by a case of glaucoma, resulted in complete blindness in one eye. Now, nearly at age 17, the cataract in Samantha's remaining good eye permits her to only distinguish between light and shadows.

Zelda spent time training new commands to Samantha while she still had a little sight left. She uses these commands to alert Samantha to obstacles in her way. "Samantha never lost her beautiful, calm personality," says Zelda. "I think this was probably because we began training while she still had some sight."

Still, it became increasingly difficult for Zelda to watch her canine companion at the park. Samantha became confused and upset when there were too many other dogs in one place. "She would panic," Zelda explains, "because she was afraid of losing me." Walks along the paved pathways became halting and hesitant. Sometimes Samantha even stumbled and fell off. She frequently needed to be picked up and carried.

Zelda realized that they needed help if they were going to continue visiting the park. "I just knew there had to be a way for this dog to go to her favorite place, be with her friends, and still enjoy the best things in her life in spite of her blindness," insisted Zelda. And so began the search.

Zelda first tried to seat Samantha in a wagon, and then a little cart. Neither was quite right. Then an Internet friend

Photo courtesy of Zelda Barnard

suggested the idea of baby stroller, and as Zelda says, "That was the ticket! I owe her a big kiss."

The first stroller Zelda purchased from a department store was a three-wheeled, all-terrain type, like one she had seen a mother pushing in the park. Unfortunately, it didn't accommodate a dog as well as it did a child, and Zelda took it back. By now she had a better idea of what she was looking for and found another all-terrain stroller, one that had four double-wheels and a back that reclined.

"The first few times I put her in the stroller she wanted to get out. She was kind of frightened by the whole thing," Zelda recalls, "but she very quickly realized it was nice to ride up that big hill receiving pats and treats along the way."

These days, when Zelda and Samantha go to the park, Samantha still spends part of the time visiting with her canine friends on her own. But now, if there is a lot of confusion, she goes immediately to her stroller, knowing she will be safe there. Then the two of them set out along

Photo courtesy of Zelda Barnard

Photo courtesy of Zelda Barnard

the trails. "It is so sweet to see her little sightless face turned upward as she takes in the all the familiar scents of the park and the ocean," says Zelda.

Other dogs often come up to the stroller to as if to say "Hi" or "What the heck is this!?" People come over to pet Samantha, which delights her. She sits upright in the stroller most of the time, but if she is very tired, she can lie down and take a nap in the sunshine. Zelda was so pleased that she was able to keep these basic pleasures in her dog's life. "It was such a simple way to give her the best of life in spite of her handicap. After all, she's given us so much pleasure, it seemed only fair."

Some people believe that blindness in dogs strengthens the human-canine bond. Clearly in this family, devotion is a two-way street.

"All love is sweet, given or returned.
Common as light is love,
and its familiar voice wearies not."

— Percy Bysshe Shelley

Look Before You Leap

The summer of 1996 was an unusually warm one in the Pacific Northwest. Sightseers and residents alike flocked to the rugged and usually bleak Oregon coastline. It was so warm that year, children even ventured into the cool ocean waters.

One popular swimming spot was at the mouth of the Necanicum River, where it entered the Pacific. This broad expanse of river made for an inviting playground. Here, the water was smooth in comparison to the crashing surf beyond it, but it belied a deadly secret: As water flowed

Photo courtesy of Joe Megaw

from the Necanicum into the Pacific, strong and unexpected currents were created.

Norman, a yellow Labrador Retriever, and his owner, Annette, frequently took trips to the beach. Like many other days, Annette was tending to her young son, Paul, and Norman was gleefully running along the shoreline with a stick in his mouth. He loved the wide-open expanse of the beach.

Photo courtesy of Annette McDonald

Unexpectedly, Norman dropped his stick, ran into the ocean, and started swimming straight into deep water. Annette, initially confused by this, quickly became frantic. She didn't know what Norman was doing, where he was going, or even, if he could swim! She called and called his name but he continued swimming away from her.

Suddenly, Annette became aware of something else. What she thought had been the joyful noises of children at play were really cries for help. A teenage girl and her younger brother had been playing in the water. Both of the children were actually very capable swimmers, but the Necanicum had become too much for them. The boy was able to make it to shore, but his sister needed help.

Annette realized what was happening. Norman must have recognized the urgent pitch in the girl's voice, and was swimming to help her. Annette shouted to the girl, "His name is Norman! Call his name!" The swimmer caught a glimpse of the dog coming toward her, and called out to him.

Norman followed the sound of the girl's voice and swam to her. She grabbed the thick fur of his ruff and together they headed in toward shore. Annette let out a sigh of relief. Everything seemed fine until the girl lost her grip and quickly became separated from Norman.

Annette hollered again, "Call his name! His name is Norman!" Again, the girl did as she was told, and she and dog caught up with each other. Finally, after what had seemed like hours, they made it to the beach.

This would be a wonderful and touching story if it had ended right there. What makes it truly amazing is that Annette and her husband, Steve, had adopted Norman from the local animal shelter the day before he was scheduled to be euthanized. Even more extraordinary than that, though, was the fact that Norman had been suffering from progressive retinal atrophy for the past two years. He was completely blind when he saved this girl from certain drowning.

When Norman started losing his vision, friends told Annette and Steve to have the dog euthanized. They were so glad they didn't listen. The same was obviously true for the children swimming in the ocean that day.

Blind dogs **can** live happy and useful lives.

"Life is mostly froth and bubble,
Two things stand in stone;
Kindness in another's trouble,
Courage in your own."

— A.L. Gordon

Blind Faith

Trinket, a beautiful, 14-year-old Cocker Spaniel, lost her sight suddenly after eye surgery. She had a difficult time adjusting to blindness, due partly to her age, and partly to its sudden onset. This normally perky little dog sank into a deep depression. Her owner, Donna, experienced feelings of loss as well. It was painful for her to watch the changes in Trinket.

Many of Donna's emotions revolved around Trinket's surgical procedure. Donna wished she had been given more information about the surgery and the possible side effects to her dog. She also worried that they would no longer be able to enjoy their favorite past time: hiking and backpacking together.

During the 14 years of little Trinket's life, she and Donna had gone trekking all around the United States. Trinket even carried her own backpack. "I remember how excited she would get whenever she saw that backpack come out of the closet," explains Donna.

"She knew we were going hiking and would launch into her going-hiking-dervish-dance! It consisted of great leaps and spinning around," smiles Donna. "I think her excitement was one of my main motivations for hiking in the first place."

Donna and Trinket had hiked in Kentucky, Colorado and Minnesota. Most often, though, they found themselves close to home in southern Indiana's McCormick's Creek State Park.

The rolling hills of southern Indiana are rugged and un-developed in places. The state park reflected this by des-ignating some of its hiking trails as "easy" and others as "moderate" in terms of difficulty. In the days before her surgery, Trinket could handle even the most arduous ones. "Big boulders, ladders, stiles, loose rock and slippery leaves were all great fun for her," says Donna.

Photo Courtesy of Donna Deter

Nearly six months after the vision loss, Trinket began emerging from her depression. She had some good days, and some bad, but Donna was beginning to see glimpses of Trinket as her "old self." Donna decided it was time to see if there was any hope of hiking together again.

One crisp day in early November, Donna put Trinket in the car and drove to the park. Donna explains, "At first I thought I would try her on an easy trail, but it didn't go very well. She lagged so far behind that it took all 16 feet of the retractable leash to keep us together." Donna was terribly disappointed. "I would take three steps and then wait. Then another three steps...well, you get the picture."

On a hunch, Donna took her to another trail. "This trail was a good bit harder, and rated 'moderate' in difficulty, but it was one we had hiked often when Trinket could still see," explains Donna. "It was one of our favorite trails, and we both knew it well."

At the head of the trail, Trinket still lagged quite a bit but continued to pick up speed as they progressed. Donna recalls, "I was still pretty concerned though, because I knew that about halfway through the trail, there was a fairly steep drop—about 60 feet. The slope was composed of large rocks, not really large enough to call boulders," Donna clarifies, "but still a big challenge for a little blind dog like Trinket."

As they neared the rocky slope, Donna gave Trinket the command: "Step." As Donna explains, "This was Trinket's cue that we were approaching a step-off." Trinket allowed Donna to guide her with the leash, and listened each time she was told to take a step.

"She handled it like a real pro. In fact, once we were at the bottom of the slope, I realized that Trinket had made it down with more confidence than when she had walked on the flat ground.

"I also realized what an enormous leap of faith I had just witnessed in Trinket. She had always been a very confident, 'take charge' kind of dog before the blindness. When we used to hike these trails, she always chose her own route over obstacles, and it was always better than the one I chose," Donna chuckles. "I finally learned to follow *her* as long as it didn't involve going under something too low, or through a spot too narrow. On that particular day, Trinket had to put her faith in me."

From that point on, Trinket just kept gathering steam. Donna could almost hear her say, "If I can conquer that, I can do anything!" The Cocker Spaniel remembered all the various spots where she had once seen grouse and pileated woodpeckers. "She knew right where to 'look' for them, and indeed, she found them," Donna recalls.

Trinket even remembered and turned onto the tight, switchback trail that branched off the main path and led them home. At the trail's end, Trinket was trotting along, reminding Donna very much of the Trinket of old. That day was a very good day for Donna and Trinket.

"There's no thrill in easy sailing
when the skies are clear and blue,
There's no joy in merely doing things
which anyone can do.
But there is some satisfaction
that is mighty sweet to take,
When you reach a destination
that you thought you'd never make."

— Spirella

Set Your Sights High

"Charlie came to me through RAGOM, the Golden Retriever rescue group I work with in Minnesota. He was found in a terrible puppy-mill situation," explains Julie, his proud new owner. "According to the ophthalmologist, he has end-stage PRA, and is totally blind."

"He lived, and I use that word loosely, in a filthy, crowded shed with 11 other dogs. Believe it or not, the puppy-mill breeder used Charlie as breeding stock!" Julie shakes her head with a mixture of disgust and disbelief. "He had never been inside a house or on a leash, and he was pretty scared of human contact."

Shortly after Charlie arrived at Julie's home, though, she began to see changes in him. "His natural Golden Retriever temperament started to come out. Even though he was blind, I decided to take him to obedience class, just as we do with many of the foster dogs."

There was another reason Julie wanted to take Charlie to obedience class. During a conversation she had with an acquaintance of hers, Julie was told that RAGOM should have just put the dog to sleep…that he wasn't good for

Photo courtesy of Tim Luchsinger

anything. Julie believed she had been issued a challenge. "I felt that Charlie would do anything I asked of him."

Every Monday evening, for the next eight weeks, Julie loaded Charlie into her car and drove the 20 miles to obedience school. The class was almost full. There were at least 15 other people in the class, training dogs of all breeds.

"I didn't want any special treatment from my classmates, so I only told the teacher about his PRA. I had a lot of faith in Charlie, and I wanted to see just what a blind dog could do." She chuckles, "No pun intended!"

During the course of classes, Charlie learned to sit, stay, lie down, heel, and come on command. Julie and the instructor also taught him a few special commands because of the blindness. Julie explains, "We taught him 'over,' which meant to move away from my voice; 'up' and 'down' for dealing with steps; and 'easy' for when something was coming up in front of him."

She continues, "As you can see, Charlie has accomplished quite a bit in such a short time. The blindness has caused him some tough moments, but on the other hand, it has also made the little accomplishments seem all the more amazing."

The night of obedience-school graduation, each dog and owner were asked to demonstrate the various exercises they had been taught. Julie admits she was a little nervous.

When Julie's turn arrived, she began by asking Charlie to sit at her left side. He did so, gladly. She told him, "Stay," and walked across the room. Julie turned back to face the dog and called "Come!" Charlie hopped up, and eagerly trotted across the room to Julie. When he reached her, he sat at her feet. Then Julie gave the command to "Finish." Charlie hopped up again, circled behind her, and sat neatly at her left side.

The class applauded loudly. The obedience instructor asked the class if anyone had noticed anything different about Charlie, or how he responded to training. The answer was a unanimous "no." When she explained Charlie's situation, the class responded in utter disbelief.

"I was so proud of him, I took it one step further," Julie giggles. "I took him for the Canine Good Citizen Test and the Therapy Dog Test. The first one evaluates a dog's basic temperament and sociability; the second one certifies a dog for therapy work in such places as retirement homes and hospitals." She continues, "He passed both tests with flying colors; and we were invited to join 'Pals on Paws', a local therapy group."

Photo courtesy of Tim Luchsinger

Julie took Charlie to a nursing home in Coon Rapids for their first therapy visit. Like many young dogs, Charlie was full of energy, dancing to and fro, as they approached the building.

Julie remembers saying to herself, "Uh oh, what have I gotten myself into?" Once inside, though, Charlie quickly realized the nature of the game and settled down.

"Charlie was *extremely* gentle with the residents. He let me lift up his front paws so the bedridden residents could pet him. Some people pet pretty hard, but Charlie happily endured it."

She continues, "Sometimes there was only enough room for Charlie to go between two beds, but not enough to turn around. I sent Charlie in with a new command of 'Forward.' When it was time to go, I said 'Back up'. He is such a smart dog."

By the end of the visit, Charlie was walking up to residents, sitting without being asked, and waiting with a smile to be petted. He did all the beneficial things therapy dogs are known for...helping people communicate, providing physical contact and mental stimulation. Julie concludes, "Therapy dogs bring a measure of healing into places that may be sparse and scary for people."

Photo courtesy of Tim Luchsinger

Julie stops for a moment to ponder what she's just said. "You know, that's funny. That's just the kind of environment Charlie came from: sparse and scary. How ironic that is. Mankind treated him so badly, and yet he's still so willing to give back compassion to people in need."

"The better I get to know man,
the more I find myself loving dogs."

— Charles DeGaulle

In Plain Sight

A volunteer from Labrador Retriever Rescue called Kathy to say that they were holding a black Lab at the local animal shelter. She went on to say that the dog had been found nearby, at the intersection of 39th Street and Oak. What she really should have said was that he was found *in* the intersection.

The dog had been lying in the middle of the pavement with his legs outstretched and his head buried beneath his paws. It was as though life had just become too difficult for this gentle spirit, and he had thrown in the proverbial towel. The only reason anyone had even helped this poor creature was that he was causing a traffic problem.

Kathy had been involved with Labrador rescue work for many years. Black Labrador males were her personal favorite. And while she fully expected that she would someday adopt a special-needs dog, she didn't realize the time was at hand.

She drove to the animal shelter unsure of what she would see. Some of these dogs were in pretty bad shape when they came in. This one was no exception. He was emaciated and disoriented. He had whipworms, kennel cough, ticks, and a bad ear infection. He was blind from PRA and tested positive for heartworms, a life-threatening condition.

"In addition to all his problems, though, there was a special sweetness about him," remarks Kathy. "I was afraid to give my heart to this little guy who might not live, but I did."

Photo courtesy of Kathy McGeever

She named him "Keller" after Helen Keller. Kathy continues, "Once you name something, it belongs to you. That's how Keller became mine."

Kathy nursed her new dog through a rocky recovery. "Keller's heartworm treatment was a trial," she remembers. "He didn't do well with it at first. He was constantly sick to his stomach and spiked a high fever." Kathy and Keller traveled back and forth to the vet and treatment finally prevailed.

Keller continued to make a profound recovery from many of his health problems, one of which was his ear infection. Kathy had created a routine of cleaning and medicating his ears at bedtime. "I would call all three of my

Labs upstairs to the bedroom with me," she explains. "Once there, I would clean Keller's ears and instill the drops. He *hated* the whole procedure. It didn't take long before he recognized the routine and tried to avoid it."

"One night I gathered all the dogs in my bedroom, all, that is, except Keller. I called and called him, but he didn't come," recalls Kathy. "I live in a small townhouse, with few places for a dog to hide, so I was a little puzzled as to where he could be.

"I went back downstairs, and as I turned the corner, I got my answer." Keller was sitting perfectly still…perfectly still and only inches away from Kathy's life-size Sandicast sculpture of a black Lab. "It was like seeing double!" Kathy laughs. "Keller was pretending he couldn't hear me, but that was impossible because I was roaring with laughter!

Photo courtesy of Kathy McGeever

"Poor Keller must have thought: 'If I just *sit next to this guy*, she won't notice me!' "

"If you pick up a starving dog and make him prosperous, he will not bite you. This is the principle difference between a dog and a man."

— Mark Twain

Looking on the Bright Side

When Kathy first told me about Keller's antics to avoid his ear medication, it made me laugh. It also pointed out a mistake I had made. When I wrote "Living With Blind Dogs," I contended that most dogs have two main functions: they announce strangers at the door and they cuddle with us. Well, that's not quite right. Dogs do something else, they make us laugh. Blind dogs are no exception.

— C. L.

Hiding next to the Sandicast statue wasn't Keller's only humorous escapade. He is also prone to hiding

Photos courtesy of Kathy McGeever

his favorite chew-toys much the same way other dogs bury a bone. In Keller's case, he tries to hide his toys from Kathy's other two Labradors, Thunder and Lightening.

Photos courtesy of Kathy McGeever

Being blind, and living with roommates for the first time, Keller frequently makes the mistake of poorly hiding his toys. As Kathy explains, "He takes his treats and chewies and 'hides' them behind a chair.

Unfortunately, the chair is in the middle of the room!" She chuckles and continues, "Thunder follows Keller and steals his treat almost every time unless I interceed. Keller now understands what I mean when I tell him, 'You better get that!' "

Stephanie trained and showed her lovely red Chow-Chow, Charlotte, well into the advanced levels of show-ring obedience. In fact, Charlotte was only one show away from earning the Canadian Kennel Club title of "Companion Dog Excellent" when she was retired from competition due to vision loss.

As Stephanie adjusted to the changes brought on by her dog's blindness, she continued to work and train Charlotte with a variety of new commands. "I think the work we had done prior to the blindness really paid off. I was familiar with positive reinforcement training, and Char and I have always had a very close relationship," explains Stephanie.

During the Christmas season the year Char went blind, Stephanie and her husband both tried to assist her, as much as they could. Stephanie explains, "My husband, Bud, had been watching me retrain Char and was doing his best to help.

Photo courtesy of Stephanie Garon

"One night, we were all watching TV. Char and her big brother, Wilbur, were dozing together in the middle of the living-room floor," recalls Stephanie. "At one point, Charlotte stood up, shook herself off, and decided to take a walk...straight into the Christmas tree. My husband and I yelled 'careful!' so loudly, an in *unison*, that we both jumped out of our chairs!" laughs Stephanie. "Char did a quick 180-degree turn and we all spent the next few minutes giggling our heads off...well, not Char, she just smiled that little Chow smile she has."

R ichard and his wife, Barbara, live on an eight-acre "gentleman's farm" in the deep woods of Piedmont, North Carolina. For 13 years, they had shared their home with Butterscotch, a parti-colored Cocker Spaniel.

"Because we were surrounded by a huge forest, we always had deer around, lots of them. Sometimes they came through the yard in whole herds. They were there almost all the time, especially in the fall," recalls Richard.

When Butterscotch was young, he was the "great protector" of his home, barking ferociously through the windows as the deer quietly milled around the yard.

"I think the reason the deer came through the yard so often was because they knew they would be safe," Richard explains. "I'm a real softy. I like all animals, so we kept Butterscotch indoors when the herds came close."

Photo courtesy of Richard Hattaway

As the years went by, Butterscotch slowly lost his vision and his hearing. He had memorized the lay of the land, both in the house and in the yard. Richard reminisces, "He knew where everything was, and spent most of his day happily wandering around in a world of his own.

"Many times, in those later years, Barbara and I looked out the window to see the funniest sight. Sometimes the deer entered the yard when Butterscotch was out there, too. Being both blind and deaf, though, he was oblivious to the them," chuckles Richard.

"The deer must have realized that Butterscotch was no longer a threat. They followed our dog, once their arch-enemy, at a distance of about 15 feet. The deer snorted and pawed at the ground, trying so hard to attract the dog's attention."

"We sat in the house and just *howled* at that sight! It wasn't that we were laughing *at* Butterscotch; it was just so funny, seeing the animals interact like that," Richard smiles.

Photo courtesy of Richard Hattaway

"He was a plucky little dog, never adversely affected by his blindness and we really loved him. I could go on and on, telling about his wild antics and memorable personality."

When Carlisle went blind, she developed the other classic symptoms that go with it. "She became both confused and depressed," explains Angele, Carlisle's devoted owner. "After two months the depression began to lift, and we were thrilled. Carlisle was still disoriented a little while longer, but every day we could see her personality re-emerging."

Angele elaborates, "I can't really say that we had 'the old' Carlisle back. Her personality had a new twist to it. Before the blindness, Carlisle was a little bit of a sissy. Ever since she went blind, though, she has been spunky and very adamant about letting us know what she wants!" Angele laughs.

Photo courtesy of Angele Fairchild

"She becomes more vocal every day," Angele continues. "If you know the Miniature Schnauzer breed, you know that they make a peculiar sound, not really a bark, but a 'woo-woo-woooooo!' Angele tries to demonstrate.

As Carlisle continued through her adjustment phase, she assisted Angele and her husband, Jim, with *their* acceptance, as well. Unbeknownst to the Miniature Schnauzer, Carlisle provided the comic relief that is so often necessary during life's emotional moments.

"We always said God sent Carlisle down to Earth to make people laugh," Jim confirms. "Even people who admit that they don't necessarily like dogs, look at her and smile. She is just such a sweet-looking, little ball of fluff."

Photo courtesy of Angele Fairchild

"One day I talked with another blind-dog owner," says Angele. "This lady told me that her dog sometimes sat in front of the floor lamp, mistaking it for her! I thought that was so funny. Then I realized, 'Hey! That's what Carlisle's been doing too,' and I had a good laugh."

Angele explains, "Carlisle has started sitting in front of the side-by-side refrigerator, and the grandfather clock in our front hall. Then she does her pay-attention-to-me-I'm-talking-to-you 'woo'."

Photo courtesy of Angele Fairchild

Angele, a slender woman of five-foot, three, seriously ponders her next thought, "Does she remember me to be huge!?"

A lthough they miss her dearly, Anne and Charles smile at the fond memories of Targa, their Labrador/Sheltie mix of 14 years.

"We used to call her a multi-talented dog," Anne explains. "Besides the blindness, Targa had diabetes, Cushings disease and spondylosis. We took the very best care of her that we could. And I think she enjoyed life very much, even though her daily routine quieted down a bit in those later years."

Photo courtesy of Anne Backus

Anne continues, "I remember one time when Targa was in the kitchen with me. It was a lazy morning and everything was very, very quiet. I had taken the garbage bag out of the trash can and placed it on the floor. I meant to take it outdoors, but other chores distracted me. Targa was fast asleep under the kitchen table, so I didn't even think twice about her bothering with it."

A smile crosses Anne's face. "Then an unmistakable rustling broke the quiet. I spun around to see Targa right in front of me, head first inside the bag of trash," Anne laughs. "I said, 'Targa!'...and the poor girl must have jumped two feet, straight up!

"We were both so surprised...Targa, because she was caught, and I, because Targa was doing such a naughty thing, right in front of my eyes! She must have assumed that if *she* couldn't see me, then *I* couldn't see her!" Anne muses, "I wonder if she thought blindness made her invisible…at least when she was up to mischief."

Anne concludes, "We have two new dogs since Targa's passing. Lacy came from the Humane Society and Holly from another shelter program. They don't replace Targa, no dog ever could. But I think that Targa, who was a shelter dog too, would have wanted us to open our hearts to others. I think she would have been glad to see us smile again."

"One can endure sorrow alone,
but it takes two to be glad."

— Elbert Hubbard

Love at First Sight

Pamela first noticed the woman at the next table because the restaurant was small and the woman was crying. Pamela glanced over the top of her menu to get a better look at her. The woman wiped her eyes as she told her sad tale to her dinner companion.

"This whole litter of puppies was born right there at the animal shelter. And we've gotten *so* attached to them, these past eight weeks. Well, all the other puppies have been adopted, but there's this last little one…it's blind, and nobody wants it. It's going to be euthanized tomorrow!"

Again she began to cry.

Pamela, who runs a historical ranch with a record of rescuing lost animals, felt she had only one choice. She rose from her seat and went to the next table. Pamela introduced herself and in her elegant English accent told the woman to bring the puppy to the ranch. "We can 'do' blind," she said.

The next day, the eight-week-old Border Collie puppy arrived. Pamela held her up to look at her. In between the puppy kisses and ferocious wiggling, Pamela examined her black and white markings. She found a dot on the back of the puppy's neck. "Perhaps we should call her Dottie."

Photo courtesy of Connie Zamora

One of the staff members recalls, "Everyone fell in love with the puppy, but I think they were also a bit daunted by the idea that she was blind. My husband is a director at the Braille Institute in Orange County, so I'm very famil- iar with blind children and their adaptability. We really weren't looking for another dog, but I agreed to take her home for a couple of days."

This is how Dottie arrived at Connie and John's home. Connie put the tiny puppy in a hand basket and John car- ried her next door to meet the people at the Braille School. The puppy was introduced to many staff members includ- ing Gena and Olivia, two youth consultants. As Connie and John explain it, "Gena and Olivia are especially gifted at their work. They are wonderful with the kids, and have a knack for making life fun for everyone." Once the puppy was in their hands, John returned to the work that beckoned from his desk. He was amused to find that each time he looked up he could see Dottie being passed from one staff member to the next, and loving the attention.

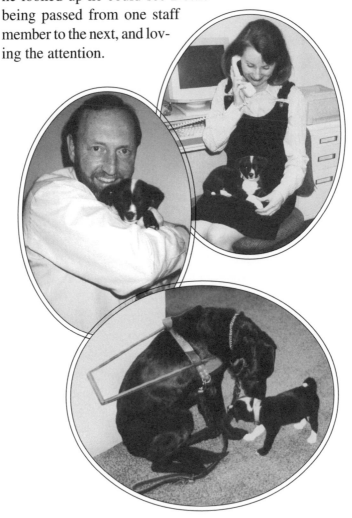

Photos courtesy of Connie Zamora

At the institute, a picture I.D. card is issued to document each person who is legally blind. Gena and Olivia were feeling particularly playful that day, and got permission from the director to hold Dottie up to the camera and make her a "Legally Blind" I.D. card too.

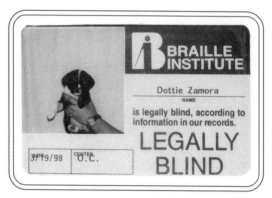

Photo courtesy of Connie Zamora

Since she had been born without eyesight, they knew she certainly qualified. The girls also thought this would be fun for the Braille students who were about to meet Dottie.

It was the teenagers who first met the puppy as they arrived for classes that day. The younger children met her the following afternoon. Many friendships were forged, as is usual among children and puppies. "The kids wanted to know how she got around and asked if she could run," explains John. "They really seemed to identify with her."

The following morning it was time to return Dottie to the ranch. Another employee had agreed to take the puppy for the weekend. Connie tied the new I.D. card to the handle of the basket and placed Dottie inside. It was then that Connie realized it was not possible for her to part with this puppy for even one day. Dottie had wiggled her way right into Connie's heart.

Photos courtesy of Connie Zamora

"She's had a big influence on the students," explains John. "One of the younger kids, being a kid, had run into something and had a scratch on his face. He asked me if Dottie ran into things. too. I told him 'Yes, she does'. Then he asked me if she cried when she ran into things. I told him, 'No, she doesn't cry.'" John smiles when he recalls how the boy raised his chin and announced, "I don't cry either."

"The kids always want to hear about her antics," John continues. "Recently, I told them how she's taken to chewing up my eyeglasses. I'm on my third

pair! It's kind of ironic, really, like she's trying to level the playing field," he laughs. "But she's just like any other dog. We're not thrilled about this, but she even hunts birds. We don't know how she does it."

As time passed, Dottie grew. She became the school mascot and a bit of a celebrity, as well. When upper-level management arrived for their annual meeting at the Braille Institute, the first question they asked was: "Where's Dottie? We'd like to meet her."

Photo courtesy of Connie Zamora

Dottie even made an occasional return trip to Rancho Los Alamitos, the ranch that first fostered her. Staff members announced: "Dottie's here. Dottie's here!"

Connie warms at the memory of how the ranch director agreed to take this doomed puppy. She remembers, too, Pamela's poignant words: "We can 'do' blind."

They certainly did.

*The most beautiful things in the world
cannot be seen or even touched.
They must be felt with the heart.*

— Helen Keller

Photo courtesy of Connie Zamora

Dottie was unexpectedly lost to heart disease during publication of this book. Her time here was short, but her influence was tremendous. — *C. L.*

A Light at the End
of the Tunnel

For most owners, it is a big day when a blind dog demon-strates his first adjustment to blindness. Small accomplish-ments are considered major triumphs. They give owners hope that life can, and will, be relatively normal for their beloved dogs.   – C. L.

Pippy came to live with AnneMarie and her husband, Gary, when she was only a year and a half old. AnneMarie explains, "Pippy came from a couple who no longer wanted her. Their baby was now a toddler, and they felt a dog was too much trouble. So Pippy, a nine-pound bundle of energy came to our house to live the life of a princess," she chuckles. "She had a long 'reign', about nine years, before she lost her sight to retinal degenera-tion."

AnneMarie continues "After Pippy was diagnosed as blind, we started the painful process of learning how to

Photos courtesy of Gary Haden

cope. At that time, Pip was banging into walls and getting lost in the house. It was difficult for us to watch."

Pippy's reaction was very typical. She became depressed and slept during much of the day. She lost interest in the daily activities around the house, as well as in her toys.

"Spring finally arrived that year, and the weather began warming up," recalls AnneMarie. "Pippy had always loved to go out in the back yard and chase the squirrels," she said, "but it didn't look like that was going to happen this year.

"She seemed to want to go out and play, but when we put her outside, she would just whine to be let back in. She was too intimidated by the steep step from the porch to the yard," AnneMarie explains. "She wouldn't budge. You would have thought we had three flights of stairs to go down. Sheesh! We were always lifting her up and down that *one* step."

AnneMarie and Gary arrived at two conclusions. They were tired of lifting Pippy up and down the step and they realized that she wasn't happy being in her yard anymore. As AnneMarie explains, "She wasn't very happy with *anything*, for that matter. Then my husband had an idea."

Gary built a short wooden ramp leading from the porch into the yard. He covered it with outdoor carpeting, and secured it to the step. AnneMarie spent the next two days training Pippy how to use it.

"I coaxed her up and down the ramp using food," says AnneMarie. "Once she understood what to do, she was racing up and down, back and forth from the porch to the yard. Now, she was whining to go *out!*" In fact, Pippy often sunbathed at the foot of her ramp, refusing to go back into the house at all.

"Within a week, Pippy's spirits lifted and she was stalking squirrels again," AnneMarie smiles. "In the old days, she obviously chased them by sight. Now, Pippy lies in the grass, very still, waiting until she hears the squirrel's chatter. She perks up her ears and makes a mad dash, just as the squirrel disappears over the top of the fence.

Photos courtesy of Gary Haden

"When Pip was first blind, I cried day and night," remembers AnnaMarie. "I tried bargaining with God to give back even a little sight to Pip. I thought she...and I...were never going to be happy again.

Photo courtesy of Gary Haden

"Those ramps were really the turning point in her adjustment, as well as mine. Pippy's blindness isn't so bad after all. Things could always be worse."

"Every day is a new experience," says Jan with a smile. "Hogan, our eight-year-old Dachshund, suddenly lost his sight from retinal degeneration. He, too, experienced the classic symptoms of depression that seem to come with it," she explains. "Six weeks after he lost his sight, my husband, Mark, and I started to see a turn-around in Hogan's behavior. He enjoyed two big achievements, one right after the other."

Jan thinks back. "I was retraining Hogan to take walks on the "pipe-leash", a special leash designed for blind dogs. He was responding well to that. Hogan seemed to be enjoying his walks more and more," she explained.

One Saturday, Jan pulled her keys out of her purse, called a good-bye to her husband, and headed toward the front door. Saturday was the day she did her grocery shopping. Just as she reached for the doorknob, she heard a flurry of activity behind her. Jan turned to see Hogan racing around the house in sheer delight.

In his excitement, Hogan repeatedly bumped into the furniture. Jan cringed each time hit something and called out, "E-e-easy!" in an effort to slow him down. "I'm sure Hogan thought I was taking him for a walk," she reminisces. "He ran to the door and then to me, then back to the door, and back to me! My husband finally picked him up so he wouldn't hurt himself. As a last resort, Hogan tried to jump out of his arms!

"That was enough for me. I decided that if our dog was so excited at the possibility of taking a walk, I could certainly make time for that," says Jan. "I put off my shopping trip for an hour and took Hogan to the park. We had a great time. When we got home, he was happy and sedate, and lay down to chew his bone.

"That was the second 'normal' thing he did that day." Jan explains. "Before the blindness he had chewed bones constantly, but not so afterwards. When he showed renewed interest in his chew-bones, we knew he was starting to adjust. We were so pleased to see him act like his old self."

Jan concludes with a smile, "Yes, every day is a new experience and they are all pretty good. I just have to be very careful now, not to jingle my keys."

"When Tyler was diagnosed with diabetes, I did some research and realized that it was a manageable disease. When he suddenly went blind, though, I really thought it was the end for him," recalls Linda, owner of the black Miniature Schnauzer sitting close to her feet.

Photo courtesy of Linda Glass

"I didn't know anyone with a blind dog at the time, and I couldn't find much information. I cried almost nonstop for two days. It was Tyler who finally helped me realize that everything was going to be okay."

Linda continues, with a frown, "Tyler suddenly went blind one September night. For many months afterwards, he was noticeably depressed. His personality had simply disappeared." Her face brightens. "Then one spring day, he was sitting on our porch, and he started barking a very special kind of bark," she laughs. "We call it the 'Cuddlesbark'!"

She reaches down to pet Tyler and elaborates, "Cuddles is another dog who lives in our neighborhood. He is the dog Tyler loves to hate." She laughs again. "I hadn't heard that bark in so many months. It was like music to my ears."

"I looked out the window fully expecting to see Cuddles and his owner, but there was no one to be seen. Tyler kept on barking. Finally, many minutes later, Cuddles and his owner came walking down the street."

Photo courtesy of Linda Glass

As if understanding the conversation, Tyler hops up and trots over to the window. "That was the first time I realized that Tyler was going to be okay," she recalls. "He must have picked up Cuddle's scent from quite a distance away, because I couldn't see anyone on the whole block." Linda shakes her head in wonder.

Tyler returns to Linda, this time, sitting *on* her feet. She continues, "From that day forward, Tyler was a different dog. It was as though he said, 'I may be blind, but this is still *my* yard!' He realized that he could still do the things he did before. We had our Tyler back again.

"After that, Tyler seemed to take on the role of blind dog public-educator." Linda stops to consider her explanation. "One day my mother and I went to the grocery store. Tyler and I stayed in the car while my mother went inside. He was on my lap hanging his head out the window, when I heard a woman cry, 'Look at the adorable Scotty!' I realized that she was confusing my Tyler with a Scottish Terrier."

"I invited the woman to come over and meet him. During our few minutes of conversation I explained that he was a Miniature Schnauzer not a Scotty, and that he was diabetic," remembers Linda. "The woman didn't know whether or not to believe me. She also didn't realize that Tyler was blind, so I told her. She kept repeating, 'That's amazing! You can't tell he's blind!'

"In the midst of the conversation Tyler became very agitated, whining and wagging his tail. I peered around the lady expecting to see my mother returning. To my amazement, I saw instead, my aunt, about 75 yards away. If I strained, I could just hear her lively chatter as she spoke with another woman."

Linda smiles at the memory. "I explained the whole situation to Tyler's new friend. It really demonstrated what amazing things blind dogs can do. I'm quite sure Tyler's new friend went home and told her family about the 'special' dog she met that day…blind but normal in so many ways."

On that note, Tyler raises himself up on his hind legs. Placing one paw on Linda's leg to balance himself, he gently gives her a kiss. Linda strokes his head, smiles and says, "I've stopped trying to figure out how or why Tyler does the things he does."

Nothing splendid
has ever been achieved
except by those who dared believe
that something inside them
was superior to circumstance."

— Bruce Barton

A Sight For Sore Eyes

Blind-dog owners commonly celebrate the first steps their dogs take toward adjustment. For a certain few, progress is especially sweet. – C.L.

Maedchen's saga with blindness began years ago. At the age of 10 months, this plucky little Shih Tzu was abandoned at a grocery store. Even then, one eye bore the signs of trauma and suspected abuse.

Fate had a mixed bag in store for Maedchen. On one hand, there would be even more hardships in store for her. On the other hand, she had the extraordinary good luck of

Photo courtesy of James Jones

being adopted by Gudrun, a woman who chuckles and explains that it is *she* who is owned by Maedchen, not the other way around.

Photo courtesy of James Jones

Gudrun and her husband, James, took Maedchen into their home and provided her with the best health care available. Initially, they had the surgeon remove the painful, traumatized eye. A year later, when a cataract matured in the remaining eye, they had the cataract surgically removed.

Sadly, fate stepped in again. Maedchen's retina detached leaving her blind in the remaining eye. She also developed glaucoma. Gudrun and James medicated her religiously, but fate played its last card. Maedchen's eye became unbearably painful and the decision was made to have it removed, as well.

"It has been a long and difficult battle," confirms Gudrun, "with many ups and downs along the way." Gudrun experienced a period of grieving, which is common among blind-dog owners, but in her case, the grieving was prolonged and profound.

Maedchen did not make an easy adjustment to blindness, either. She no longer slept through the night and withdrew from activity around the house. She developed the alarming habit of rhythmically banging her head against Gudrun's bed frame. All of this was devastating to Gudrun and compounded her grief.

Finally, after two years, life began returning to normal. Maedchen started sleeping through the night. She explored the house more and more. And she even showed renewed interest in chasing the cats off the couch again.

"All of this seemed to coincide with my new-found level of acceptance," Gudrun explains. "I've reached a point where I'm learning to accept all the things she still *can* do and not focus so much on the past. I think I might have actually been holding her back."

Gudrun turns introspective. "We live very close to the beach, so close, in fact, that you can see it from our back door. "Before she went blind, Maedchen absolutely loved the beach. It was one of her favorite places. Afterwards though, I just couldn't bring myself to face those old memories. As close as we are to the beach, I couldn't take her back there."

She elaborates, "I was so afraid of how she might react…afraid that *she* would be afraid. I thought I would spend the whole time crying and I didn't want to waste a beautiful, sunny day that way."

Maedchen continued to make progress around the house. She rediscovered her toy basket and its contents. Her antics made Gudrun laugh. She realized that her beloved dog really was adapting to blindness. Gudrun made a momentous decision. Trusting in her dog, Gudrun decided that it was time to take a trip to the beach.

Even though they could see the beach from their house, Gudrun and James loaded Maedchen into the car and drove a few minutes to their favorite spot on the Washington coast. Gudrun carried Maedchen from the parking lot onto the sand. With a mixture of fear and fond memories, she set Maedchen down.

Photos courtesy of James Jones

Surpassing all of Gudrun's expectations, Maedchen lifted up her head, took in the scents, and briskly trotted off. She appeared unconcerned with the screeching seagulls that circled and dove around her; and was indifferent to the groups of strangers strolling and chatting along the shore. Gudrun clamped her hand over her mouth as a cry of surprised delight escaped.

With intense concentration, Maedchen marched over rocks and past washed-up logs. She plowed ahead fearlessly. The family stayed on the beach for three blissful hours.

Photo courtesy of James Jones

"It was so beautiful to watch her walk without fear," remembers Gudrun. "Odd as this may seem, it was as though she followed our footsteps in the sand. I've never seen her walk in a straight line like that around the house."

She didn't realize that Maedchen had quickly learned to rely on another special canine skill. Maedchen was "tracking" her people, much as bloodhounds do.

As they neared the parking lot, a man and his small son approached them. Gudrun recalls, "The man asked me if

Maedchen was deaf. He noticed that she was holding her head up high. When I explained that, in fact, she was blind, he went on to tell me that his grandmother had owned a small terrier when he was a boy. The dog had gone blind at age 11 and lived happily to the ripe old age of 17. Hearing that made me feel as good as you can imagine."

Photo courtesy of James Jones

"On the drive home, I replayed the day's events in my head. What wonderful new memories I had!" Gudrun smiles. "Last year, I hated every ray of sunshine because I knew Maedchen would never see the sun again. This year, I'm looking forward to the summer. I might actually have to become a beach bum. What a shame that would be," she laughs facetiously.

Gudrun's face takes on a more earnest expression. "People said there would be a brighter tomorrow and they were right. It is here at last."

Self-trust is the essence of heroism.

— Ralph Waldo Emerson

Perfect Vision

Gail and her family own Crackers, an 11-year old, male Miniature Poodle. Crackers lost his sight due to diabetic cataracts, yet he still retained his role as friend and guardian. His transition to blindness was a poignant experience for Gail. And the event caused her to reflect on her own life, Crackers' life and society's reaction to the concept of being handicapped.

Photo courtesy of Chris Smith

Gail begins, "When I was a kid, I had a very serious case of the measles. It left me hard of hearing in both ears. Forty years ago, society just didn't know what to do with people like me. The thinking back then was, 'Put deaf people in a home. They won't be functional adults.'

"Society also seemed to have a hold on the direction my life would take. People drew a box around me and said, 'She can't hear. She won't be able to do this, she won't be able to do that,'" Gail reflects. "In other words, they focused on what I couldn't do, rather than what I *could* do.

"Thankfully, my parents wouldn't have anything to do with that kind of thinking. They sent me to professional speech and hearing therapy. When that was over, they continued the therapy at home, every single day.

"Oh, the stories I could tell you!" Gail chuckles. "There were hours spent with my brother on the street corner. He helped me learn to tell which way the cars were coming from. There were hours spent practicing word pronunciation, too!"

Gail continues, "Sure, I may not be able to hear the early-morning birds, or the leaves rustling in the autumn. And yes, I may have to do things a little differently than others, but it doesn't mean anything's wrong, or bad. It just means that I grew up at a time when society was uninformed."

"I don't like the labels that society bestows on those who are unlike the general population. Take, for example, the word 'handicapped'...really, now...what exactly does 'handicapped' mean?" A smile spreads across Gail's face. "Isn't there such a thing as a golf handicap? I know a few people who vie to have a measurable golf handicap!" she laughs.

"Seriously, life hasn't been all that difficult...different, yes...difficult? No. It's been creative, challenging, and certainly worth living. I think the same is true for Crackers. Like me, he has a lot to offer. Blind dogs are resilient and adaptable. They just need an educated society and willing owners.

"After telling you this story of 40 years ago, it seems absurd that people could have been so naïve back then. It makes me realize just how important it is to be informed. In a way, both my hearing loss and Cracker's blindness have had the same oddly positive effect. They've taught me to ignore the labels that people use. It's made my life so much richer and fuller."

Gail concludes, "Crackers has taught me a lot about not giving up, regardless of the circumstances. He's always been here for me, both before the blindness and after. Naturally, I will be here for him, too. How many of us can say we have such a support system?"

*"If you have knowledge,
let others light their candle at it."*

— Margaret Fuller

Other Books by the Author

"Living With Blind Dogs: A Resource Book and Training Guide for the Owners of Blind & Low-Vision Dogs"

8.5"x 11" paperback, 182 pp,, illust., ISBN 0-9672253-0-2

Helpful hints from dozens of blind-dog owners. Topics include dealing with loss, causes of blindness, how dogs react to blindness, pack interactions, helping dogs negotiate the house, yard and neighborhood, training new skills, toys & games. **Price:** $29.95 plus shipping & handling $5.95 (U.S. & Can.), $15.95 outside N. America

"Dogs, Diet and Disease: An Owner's Guide to Diabetes Mellitus, Pancreatitis, Cushing's Disease & More"

8.5"x 11" paperback, 181 pp., illust., ISBN 0-9672253-2-9

Indepth instructions to help owners care for chronically ill dogs. Discusses numerous metabolic/digestive/endocrine and immune system processes, diet, nutrition, insulin injections, Cushing's (& SARD) treatments, liver, kidney, bladder issues & more. **Price:** $29.95 plus shipping & handling $5.95 (U.S. & Can.), $15.95 outside N. America

Shipment is by Priority Mail: 1-3 day delivery in the U.S.
For credit card orders, please phone, fax, or visit our website. Make checks payable, (in U. S. funds, on U.S. banks, please) and mail to:

Caroline Levin
Lantern Publications
18709 S. Grasle Road
Oregon City, OR 97045-8899 USA

phone and fax: (503) 631-3491
email: publisher@petcarebooks.com
website: http://www.petcarebooks.com